The
SPUR BOOK
of
BACK PACKING

The
SPUR BOOK
of
BACK PACKING

by
ROBIN ADSHEAD

SPURBOOKS LIMITED

FOR THE BACKPACKERS CLUB:
— my friends, present and future.

Published 1976 by
SPURBOOKS LIMITED
6 Parade Court
Bourne End
Bucks

ISBN 0 904978 69 9

Printed by Maund & Irvine, Ltd., Tring, Herts.

CONTENTS

PUBLISHER'S INTRODUCTION

Venture Guides aim to provide outdoor enthusiasts, and all those involved in active outdoor leisure pastimes, with a range of knowledge on which to base their activities.

Whatever the particular activity, climbing, camping, rambling, sailing or whatever, the outdoor man or woman needs to have a grounding in outdoor techniques, such as Knot Tying, Boat-handling, Weather Lore, Camping Skills, First Aid, Map and Compass work and, the subject of this book, Backpacking.

And now a word about this book from the author . . .

ABOUT THIS BOOK

Every year, the pace of life in Britain gets faster, with more and more concrete covering the countryside. The traffic increases, the press of people becomes more of a burden, and the average citizen needs time to recreate a sense of peace and fulfilment that is harder and harder to find within the confines of city or factory.

The countryside of Britain is still there, and vast areas of wild country are still available to the walker. The foot is now the best form of transport for carrying the visitor into this remaining countryside. Only on foot can one get away from the television and the traffic into the quiet of the hills. Only by taking all your needs with you on your back can you remain in the green places without returning to the ties of fixed accommodation. Only by training and experience combined can you select the basic minimum of equipment with which to remain for long periods in the open country, warm, safe and comfortable.

Backpacking is the word used to describe this method of prolonging country walks by carrying all your daily needs on the back. The Backpacker is, basically, a lone traveller, independent and free from normal constraints, who uses his skill and equipment to enjoy leisure time in the country, either on a walking weekend, or a full-fledged journey.

Travelling with the minimum of well-chosen gear demands a knowledge of all the equipment now on offer. Of this, some is really ideal, designed for the specialist by the specialist. Other items are merely an attempt by some manufacturers to get a foothold in a growing market. The safest method of getting started into Backpacking is to take it all very slowly, buying equipment cautiously and only when you find the exact piece of kit you need. Quality equipment that will prolong your outdoor enjoyment

6

costs money. We tend to get exactly what we pay for. The opportunity for cutting corners in price are very few, and it is easy enough to go wrong. A well-assembled pack of equipment is an intensely personal thing, reflecting the owner's life style. Many well-intentioned would-be backpackers try to get it all together at once, and generally regret a large portion of their initial purchases once they have acquired a little more experience.

The aim of this book is to try to give information on the basic requirements of Backpacking, with a little about the techniques of all-weather camping and walking. There is virtually no limit on the money you could spend on gear, but there is a definite limit on how much weight you want to be carrying at any one time. This book is therefore aimed at the lone backpacker, but suggests, wherever possible, ways of making further savings on weight and equipment by sharing with a partner.

Most beginners are drawn to Backpacking without truly knowing why they respond so strongly to what is regarded by many as a rather odd thing to do. After all, we spend most of our lives trying to buy a house, and getting a good job. Why should anyone then want to leave the house and the normal way of life and go off into the countryside to live in a tent for a night, a weekend, or longer periods? It's not for me to give you an answer. The reasons are different for each individual. However, this book will give you a base from which to begin collecting your own experiences. The fact that you are reading this means that there is already something in Backpacking that appeals to you. If so, welcome, fellow addict, and I hope this book will make your walking easier.

SUGGESTED KIT LIST

(To be treated as a list from which to make a selection, rather than as a comprehensive list to be used in all circumstances.)

SHELTER
Tent, poles, pegs and spares.
Spare guy line.
INSULATION
3 mm underlay.
Karrimat or Adsmat.
Space blanket.
Sitzmat. (short length of
  Karrimat.)
SLEEPING GEAR
Sleeping bag.
Helly-Hansen suit.
Lifa underwear.
Devold "Hotsocks".
Helly-Hansen socks.
WARM GEAR
Balaclava hat.
Gloves or mittens.
Socks, loopstitch and thin wool.
Synthetic duvet or sweater.
Synthetic waistcoat.
CLOTHING
Tweed trousers.
Wool shirt.
String vest.
Sweater.
Boots.
RAINGEAR
Rain jacket.
Rain trousers or chaps.
Gaiters.
COOKING GEAR
Stove and fuel.
Funnel for fuel bottle.
Cookset.
Handle for cookset.
Spoons.
Tin opener.
Lighter and matches.
Windscreen.

Washing-up gear.
Washing-up towel.
ACCESSORIES
Compass and whistle.
First-aid kit.
Water containers.
Water purifying pills.
Candle.
Torch and batteries.
Knife.
PERSONAL ITEMS
Plastic mug.
Comb.
Lipsalve.
Washing kit: Toothbrush,
  paste, soap, towel.
Paper handkerchieves.
Writing paper.
Pen.
Camera, lenses, flash, film,
  tripod and other gadgets.
Radio (your choice—not mine)
Binoculars.
Paperback book.
Maps.
Toilet paper.
FOOD
Breakfasts.
Lunch items.
Main meals.
Brewkit, in containers.
Trail snacks.
Reserve meal, or survival
  food.
EMERGENCY GEAR
Money.
Credit cards.
Change for telephone.
Blood group card.
Personal medication.

Chapter 1

FOOTWEAR AND CLOTHING

The walker is dependent on his feet for transport, and nothing is more calculated to bring him up all standing than a pair of aching "dogs". Feet that hurt take all the pleasure out of backpacking, and it is therefore the Backpacker's prime responsibility to ensure that his feet are properly cared for.

SOCKS

Well-chosen socks will go a long way to making feet comfortable, keeping them warm and helping to prevent blistering. There is no substitute here for any solution less than the best, and the best means Wool. A wool/fibre mixture is acceptable, but the wool must predominate. Nylon socks will overheat the foot and should not be considered. Whether you wear one pair of thick socks, one pair of thin ones with a thicker pair over, or even two pairs of thick woollen socks is up to you. I wear two pairs of socks, always, when backpacking. The inner pair is thin wool and the outer thick pair are Loopstitch, so called because the inside of the sock is formed into a pattern of raised loops that provide a unique absorbent surface for the foot. Thicker socks called Raggsocks are favourites with many walkers.

Two pairs of socks help to reduce the likelihood of blisters forming because the surfaces of the socks absorb the chafing that would otherwise occur on the skin. In my experience, the conditions most likely to produce blisters fast are to put the feet into badly-fitting boots, wear thin socks and work up a sweat quickly. As the heat rises in the boot, "hot spots" will be caused by friction, producing a local tenderness. "Moleskin", a sort of hairy sticking plaster, can be used at this stage to prevent the "hot spot" from turning into a fully-fledged blister. Cut a patch rather larger than the painful area, round off the corners of the patch and stick it firmly down over the area, leaving it in place until it falls off.

To prevent blistering occurring, it is helpful to keep the feet dry. By changing the socks frequently, and airing the feet while changing the socks, the heat will be reduced and blisters will be kept to a minimum.

FIGURE 1

BOOTS

Well-fitting boots go a long way in protecting the feet and ensuring comfortable walking. The simplest way to start backpacking is to go for a walk in the country wearing a well-used pair of shoes or boots with a sole that will afford a reasonable grip. Walking without a load on one's back is a different thing to carrying a pack for you are adding an extra stone or two to your weight when you heft the pack on, and this weight has suddenly to be borne on your suffering feet, which are unused to the extra burden. Properly designed boots will cushion the shock, support the feet when this extra unaccustomed load is added to the normal body-weight and, with soles stout enough, protect the toes, soles and heels from the stones and flints on the path. (Figure 1)

The walker's boot should ideally be as light as possible within the requirements laid down above. The feet must be able to breathe and ventilate to avoid excessive build-up of heat, which leaves leather, in spite of the cost, as the only viable material for a Backpacker's footwear. The sole should be capable of affording a decent grip on all surfaces, and the standard satisfactory sole today is a Vibram-type composition sole. This is fastened onto a mid-sole of leather, and in the heavier types of walking boot there are two mid-soles for added firmness and stiffness to prevent the sole twisting under the walker's weight.

The height of the boot should generally be enough to cover the ankle bone, and the sides of the boot may be padded with insulating foam to give both protection and insulation around the top of the foot. The main part of the boot should be cut from one piece of leather and there should be a sewn-in tongue, padded for extra comfort. This seals in the area under the laces which should fasten with either D-rings or speed hooks. To stop bits of rock and heather coming in at the ankle, some boots are fitted with a soft roll of padded leather called a "scree cuff".

Vibram soles come in various grades. The softest is the *Securite*, which has a different pattern of sole to the heavier varieties which start with the *Roccia and Rocciablock*. These are found on light trail boots, and in my opinion are not strong enough for general all-round backpacking use. Next up are the Black, and then the Yellow Label Vibram soles, of which the best has the name MONTAGNA. This is a hard, all-purpose, long-life sole.

FIGURE 2

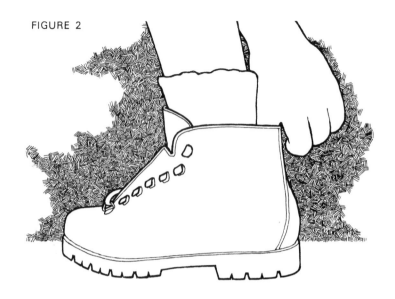

FITTING BOOTS

When buying boots, go to a specialist camping and climbing shop where an expert can ensure that you get a good fit. Wear the socks you will use for walking, and if you plan to use the two-sock method, wear both of them and tell the fitter your normal shoe size. When you put on a boot, and *before* you do up the laces, push your foot as far into the boot as you can, so that your toes are rubbing the end of the boot inside the toecap. Then try to put a finger down the inside of the heel. If there is just room for your finger behind the heel, the boots are adequately long for you, and when you tighten the laces your foot should be held into the back of the boot. When coming downhill, this added length will ensure that your toes are not banging into the end of the boot, causing pressure blisters under the toenails. (Figure 2)

The laces should be done up firmly, but not tightly, and there should still be a gap left over the instep, so that the leather can allow for stretching and still not totally close the top under the laces. There should be no feeling of constriction over the broad part of the foot, and the toes should have room to move independently. When you walk up and down in the shop, the heel should be held fairly firmly in the back of the boot, not rising more than an eighth to a quarter of an inch. Any more rise than that and you should try a smaller boot.

When you are a beginner, it would be as well to buy a pair of Army boots, as they are strong and hard-wearing, although made on an excellent last. By the time you wear them out you will know exactly what you require in your next pair of boots. Do not buy climbing boots unless you plan to use them for climbing; they will be heavier and stiffer than you need. Top weight for backpacking boots would be about 5 pounds a pair, 4-4$\frac{1}{2}$ lbs being better. Remember that an extra pound on the feet is equivalent to another five pounds on the back at the end of the day, so try to avoid burdening yourself with heavier boots than you need. Judge the type of backpacking you will be doing, in terms of terrain. The harder the ground, the more you will need a stiff sole capable of withstanding the sharpest of stones underfoot. Heather and bracken, stones and scree take their toll of a boot, and, indirectly, the foot inside.

BREAKING-IN THE BOOTS

Breaking-in a pair of boots is a subject on which opinions tend to vary. You should give the new boots time to adjust themselves to the shape of your foot before trying to do any walk longer than one down to the shops and back. This can be done by wearing them around the house, and doing short walks in the local area. As the boots become worn-in, make the training walks longer until you can do a normal unloaded day's hike without any discomfort. Then start carrying a light pack, and work up to the full load gradually. Keep the boots clean and apply a regular light covering of a good wax or leather treatment such as Hydrolan.

Should you have to do a rather more sudden breaking-in of new boots, the only rapid way I can recommend is to run the tap until hot water comes out just hot enough to make you remove your hand from under the flow. Fill one boot with the hot water, and allow it to stand for *ten seconds* only, before pouring the water straight into the *other* boot. Give that one ten seconds and then pour the water away. Drain both boots and put them on over your regular walking socks, then go out and walk them dry. All you have done is to simulate the actions of a long day's hike with hot, sweaty feet. Above all, do *NOT* soak the boots overnight in water or anything else, do *NOT* dry them out in front of the fire or by any heat other than room_ temperature air, and do *NOT* cover them in oil. As for that old saw about dubbin rotting the stitching of a boot, I cannot confirm or deny it. Before I knew about Hydrolan however, I used dubbin for my boots, and never had any rotten stitching coming adrift.

Good boots will repay many times over the care you lavish on them.

CLOTHING

Backpackers walk and camp throughout the year, enduring the worst as well as the best of the weather. By choosing the correct clothing, the body can be kept in a comfortable state.

The body produces warmth like a furnace, and this warmth is dispersed from the surface of the body through the skin. In hot weather clothing must be chosen to dissipate this heat and to keep the body temperature down. Loose clothing, light and airy weaves of cloth, shorts and a sunhat all help to ventilate and insulate the body from the heat even under conditions of maximum exertion. In warm weather, air must be induced to flow over the skin so that the air-cooled sweat will chill the surface of the body. When the temperature goes down, the body will shut down the sweating process. To keep the shirt off the back and help the skin to breathe, a string vest is the basic garment, covered by a shirt of open weave, with an open collar. Long sleeves that can be rolled down are useful to the backpacker when insects bite, or on the sudden onslaught of colder weather.

In really hot conditions, shorts make walking enjoyable, but when the wind begins to rise and the cool air starts to move, the backpacker is better off wearing breeches or long trousers. Even in summer in the British Isles, it is wise to be prepared for cold weather, and I use long trousers rather than breeches and stockings—only personal preference, I hasten to add. Many back-packers and walkers prefer stockings and breeches. Never wear jeans, as they are chilly and uncomfortable when wet.

The condition more usual to the British backpacker is that of being too cold rather than too hot. In this case, loss of body heat must be avoided by covering the body with clothing in several thin layers rather than one thick one. The barrier that prevents heat loss is actually the layers of still, dry air which are kept in place by the clothing. The first of these barriers is once more created by the string vest, over which is worn either a thin, lamb's wool sweater, or a wool shirt. The lamb's wool sweater is exceedingly efficient as an insulator, but tends to get a bit smelly over a period of days of exertion. To the same degree, a shirt will also tend to absorb sweat, but an open shirt has the advantage of being ventilated down the front.

Another thin sweater can then be worn over the shirt. Warm air is trapped in the holes of the string vest, and although warmed air is constantly on the move, the string holds it from moving from the surface of the body, thus retaining the warmth. The sweater or shirt creates another layer, and the next layer does the same. Over the top, in really cold, dry climates and conditions goes a garment made of breathable nylon, stuffed with down or man-made fibre, very light and compressible. Depending on actual temperatures, this can be either a "down sweater", a lightweight filled coat or a full-blooded mountain 'duvet' jacket. These together will probably be sufficient for average winter conditions.

INSULATION

The use of down for insulation gives the backpacker the finest compromise of light weight, compressibility and warmth retention. The down, lofting in its nylon cover, creates many tiny pockets of still, dry air, which, as I have said before is the finest insulation you can get. This state continues until the down gets wet; it then clumps together, becomes soggy, and loses most of its efficiency to insulate. Wet weather makes down quite useless.

At this point, man-made Fibrefill and P3 fibres take over. These are nylon or terylene strands, made, in the case of Fibrefill 2 out of short lengths held together by crimping, and in the case of P3 as an endless filament laid back and forth to form a mat which is then quilted into usable material. These nylon fibres have virtually no water-absorption capability and will retain their in-built loft even when soaking wet. For use in wet-cold conditions, they have the edge over the much more expensive down as a filling for backpackers' garments. To get the best combination of warmth retention by multi-layered clothing, my own choice is now (1) a waistcoat made of Fibrefill 2, then (2) a long-sleeved sweater of the same material with an optional clip-on hood. This combination garment gives the maximum number of options through all seasons, and has the added advantage that it packs into different spaces in the pack. In summer, the waistcoat may be used alone, the sweater used alone in autumn and spring, with or without the hood, and the whole lot used together in the depths of winter. With a thick one-piece duvet jacket though the options are only to have it on or off, or open or shut, so my combination is preferable.

The ability of man-made fibres to retain body heat when wet

makes them a good choice to wear under the outer, clothing which should be both wind and rain-proof. The worst conditions that a backpacker can meet will combine cold and wet weather with high, chilling winds. These conditions when met all at once can be lethal. (See Chapter 12, on Hazards.) Unfortunately our technology has not yet produced the ideal material for a back-packer's outer shell clothing, as the ideal would have to be both totally breathable while remaining totally waterproof. So far these two requirements are incompatible.

OUTER GEAR—RAIN WEAR

The backpacker slogging along with his raingear firmly closed up against the elements must slow down in order to void over-heating inside the sealed shell of his raingear. In effect he is making his own mini-climate inside by producing quantities of warm, humid air which must be allowed to escape if he is to avoid making his clothing damp by virtue of his own body-moisture. Like a kettle in a warm kitchen, the body goes on churning out excess heat, which proceeds outwards until it comes across a barrier through which it cannot pass. Because of the rain beating against the outside of the raingear, its surface is chilled like the kitchen window, and the warm air inside the rain jacket is suddenly cooled below its "dew" point. The moisture content becomes too much for the volume of air it is in, and so it turns back into condensation on the inside of the water proofs.

The beginner, stripping off his rain jacket after a few miles of this sort of thing is convinced that the jacket has been letting in the rain. This is not so, and it is equally wrong to assume that because the water drops have soaked back into your outer layers of clothing, making them sodden and uncomfortable, you would have been just as badly off had you possessed no outer shell clothing at all. In fact, you are a lot better off, because it is better to be warm and wet inside your shell garments, than wet and chilled without them. The mini-climate inside your raingear protects and conserves your body heat for longer than would be possible had you no shelter from the chilling wind and rain at all. You will be warm and wet inside the shell clothing, rather than very cold and wet without it. That can in the worst instances be a difference between life and death. Put like that, you can see that your raingear begins to assume a considerable importance; it pays to invest in a really good suit of raingear that is waterproof, and which will go on being waterproof.

Another type of material to wear *under* the outer raingear is fibre pile. Garments made of this fluffy nylon can be obtained as

FIGURE 3

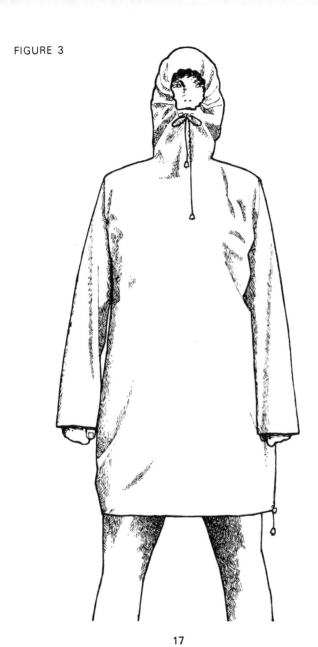

waistcoats, pullovers, sweaters and even one-piece suits. The backpacker, seeking as many applications as possible for his single item of clothing will most likely go for the zip-front sweater-type garment with sleeves. In wet, warm weather, this will suffice by itself as something to wear all day under the rainwear.

CAGOULES AND OVERTROUSERS

The simplest type of raingear is the cagoule, an all-enveloping tube of a coat having a full hood with drawstrings, and another drawstring round the bottom of the coat. This voluminous mini-tent is NOT the backpacker's ideal rainproof clothing as the options are only to have it on or off. Better by far is a long jacket that will open down the front with a two-way zipper. Options then increase for maximum ventilation without removal of the shell. Pockets, if there are to be any, should be sunk fairly low on the jacket to allow use of a padded hip belt on the backpack, (See Chapter 6), and they should have a good flap or they will fill up with water. (Figure 3)

Overtrousers complete the set of outer raingear. They can be anything from chaps, which are merely tubes of waterproof nylon or other material which are pulled on over the boots and tied up on to the belt, leaving the crotch free of covering, to a sophisticated pair of full trousers with gussets at the ankle closed by zippers, and a vented waistband to let out the steamy air. The backpacker should assess his probable needs and then look for the complete range of raingear in a specialist outfitters.

GAITERS

Additional items are the short gaiter, or "Stop-Tous", and the full, knee-length gaiter. Both types fasten at the back or side with a zipper, and tie under the instep of the boot with cords. The aim of the short gaiter is only to seal the top of the boot and prevent any loose stones and bits of heather and grass from penetrating the inside of the boot to irritate the foot. The long gaiters keep the ankle and calf well protected from thorns, gorse, heather and bracken, and are exceedingly useful items of equipment. Not only do they keep your trousers dry when walking through long wet grass after a shower, but they can be used as waterproof seats, as tablecloths for laying out food, as covers for boots in the tent at night, and even as windscreens for the stove. I would rather have my gaiters with me than the overtrousers if it came to a choice.

HEADGEAR

A last word about raingear should include mention of the hood of the jacket. Most of these hoods are cut to accommodate a climber's helmet, and are thus on the full side. This is useful when the backpacker wears a woolly hat or balaclava. The ideal hood should have a wire or other form of light stiffener which pulls out the front of the hood to form a peak or tunnel to protect the face and nose from wind and driven rain or snow. A hood that simply closes with a drawstring around the face is not sufficient in my opinion.

Up to 30% of the body's heat loss is through the head, and if the neck and shoulders are included, this rises to 60%. It is therefore vital to have some form of head covering, preferably wool, with which to reduce this loss. The best form of hat that I have found, and one which I carry the year round, is the pure wool balaclava helmet that can be pulled down to make a scarf. In the raised position, this scarf forms a double thickness of wool over the ears, and is very comforting in a cold wind. The helmet can be used at night in a sleeping bag to give additional warmth retention to the head and neck.

OTHER ITEMS

Other extremities that need their own covering are the hands. Gloves or mitts are another item to carry in all seasons, although the winter ones should obviously be heavier. The wool mitt is a good starting point, but I have found the fibre pile mitts to be capable of keeping my hands warm even when they are wringing wet. In snow, or heavy rain, a light nylon waterproof overglove is a useful addition, but I never seem to carry them nowadays. In rain, it is easier to pull the hands up into the long sleeves of the rain jacket, and it is one thing less to carry.

I like to hold up my trousers with a belt, but when a hip belt is worn over the top, the trouser belt must be hitched up out of the way. To avoid discomfort, I try to keep as little as possible in my pockets, restricting their contents to a handkerchief where I can. Sometimes a small knife is carried there, though it is usually on my belt. A lighter or small coins can be carried for easy access, but there are better ways to carry these items, without rubbing sores on your legs. I wear a scarf round my neck that serves as a towel, pot holder, sweat rag and anything else I need from a bandage to a washing-up cloth. After several days, it is not very sociable and needs a wash-out. Being cotton, it dries quickly.

Chapter 2

SLEEPING BAGS AND SHELTER

We go backpacking to enjoy the journey, or merely to be in the open air again. We have already seen that sore feet can ruin an otherwise good trip; so can a bad night's sleep. The most efficient way to get a good night's rest is to sleep in a properly designed backpacker's sleeping bag, and you should not economise on this item. Get a really good bag, and it will serve you well for 10 to 15 years. A poor one with useless filling will hardly endear itself to you when you awake cold in the middle of a freezing night. At this point all the fivers in the world laid end to end will not keep you warm. Remember who will be sleeping in the bag before you buy a cheap one.

The aim of a good sleeping bag is to wrap the sleeper in an efficient form of insulation that will preserve body heat by creating a barrier of warm, still air between his body and the cold night air. It is not the filling that provides the warmth; the filling just provides the still air layer. The efficiency of any filling is judged by the amount of still air space it can provide per unit of its weight. For the backpacker looking for a top quality bag there are only two fillings worth bothering about; waterfowl down, and man-made fibre.

DOWN

This comes from geese or ducks, and is their undercoat, not the top feathers. It is the most efficient insulator of all as far as sleeping bags are concerned. It is capable of being compressed over and over again into a tiny space, and when released will loft up to its original volume, creating thousands of little dead air spaces that insulate the sleeping body. It has the property of being breathable, and can get rid of the body's exhalations of warm moist air without absorbing it. Wet down, however, loses most of its insulating ability rapidly, so a down sleeping bag must *at all times be protected from damp and moisture.*

The chances of getting a goosedown bag nowadays are few, and most of the top-quality bags are made of new white duck down. A small proportion of feathers are included with the pure down to preserve the lofting power of the bag, that is, its capacity to revert to its normal insulation thickness when not under compression. Any bag that is described as being "down and feather mixture", or worse, "feather and down mixture", or worst of all, makes no mention of the word "down", is of very limited use to the backpacker, who looks for the most efficient, light and most compressible gear. These feather bags reflect their quality in their lower price and greater weight and bulk. You get what you pay for.

MAN-MADE FIBRE
These synthetic fillings for most backpacking purposes can be limited to two. These are Fibrefill 2, a second-generation dacron that is made from short lengths of filament matted together and quilted, and P3, another soft fibre made from endless lengths of filament laid over and over itself before being quilted for ease of cutting and handling. While being neither so efficient in insulating nor so light and compressible as down, these fibres have distinct advantages to the all-weather British backpacker in that they are much cheaper to buy, need no particular care in use and can keep the sleeper adequately warm even when they are soaking wet, thanks to their very limited water absorbency. Should a fibre bag become wet, the sleeper has merely to wring it out and get back inside where he will keep clammy but warm; the same cannot be said of down. My own belief is that with the rising price of down, these bags will tend to increase in sophistication and efficiency, while remaining at prices that most of us can afford. For general British conditions, I would wholeheartedly recommend them to the backpacking beginner making his first purchase. Down bags are for the purist looking for the very best and lightest gear, and who has more money to spend. (Figure 4)

Synthetic bags have been in use in America for about 5 or 6 years, and long-term users there report that the life of a fibre bag is not to be reckoned in the same terms as down. Prolonged compression in a stuff sack will decay the fibre's lofting capacity in the long run, thus reducing the insulating air space.

MATERIALS AND DESIGN
The most common covering for sleeping bags today is nylon taffeta or ripstop. Taffeta is a smooth surface, lightly coated to assist in the retention of the down, while rip-stop cloth has a raised heavy thread woven in every $\frac{1}{4}$ inch or so to help in containing any accidental tear or puncture. Ripstop is more fashionable than plain taffeta, which can be made to the same tear strength and thread count, and which will perform the same job.

21

FIGURE 4

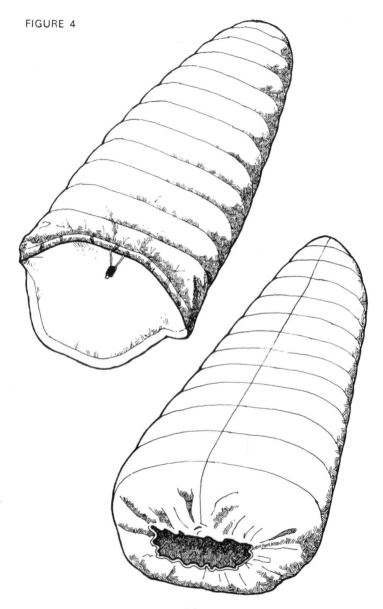

BAG-SHAPE

A backpacker's sleeping bag must be cut with the same aims of *efficiency* and *lightness* as the remainder of his kit. There should be no spare space in the bag to require his precious body heat to warm it, and the resulting slim-cut bags may feel restricting at first. To conserve weight and insulating efficiency, the full-length zippers used in American sleeping bags are generally left out of British-made bags, which are usually entered from the neck. There should be a well-shaped hood that can be pulled over the head, with a draw-string to keep it in place. This helps to prevent body heat loss from the head, neck and shoulders. The sleeper's feet will feel compressed unless a boxed foot is incorporated, allowing proper insulation around the end of the bag.

Some makers cut the inside of a bag slightly smaller than the outer cover. This method is called differential cut. (The other method is to make both inner and outer cover the same size.) In theory this gives less opportunity to the sleeper to touch the outer wall of the bag, thus causing heat loss; in my experience, I have never noticed any particular advantage with either cut.

STITCHING

The simplest way to hold the insulation in position without it constantly shifting is to stitch it into boxes or sleeves wth a straight-through stitch. Heat may be lost through the stitching, so this method is reserved for summer use bags. If however another simple-quilted bag is placed *inside* the first, so that the lines of stitching do not match up with one another, the heat loss is prevented. This method is called the "double garment" principle, and results in a warm, efficient but rather heavy bag, due to the extra cloth used in construction.

To allow the filling the maximum loft, walls are put between the covers of the bag to create boxed areas of fill. These walls are called "baffles" and are made of very light netting which stop the down from migrating all over the bag when it is shaken out. Baffles can be simple box, slant-walled or V-shaped. The simple box is more than adequate for all-year-round bags, while the slant-wall is just an added refinement that works. V-baffling is best left to expedition-type bags because of the extra cost of construction and the extra weight. In Britain the good makers favour either small baffles that hold the down in place, or larger baffles that really let the down reach its maximum loft. Although I favour the latter, I have slept warm in both types, and would say only that

SIMPLE QUILTING

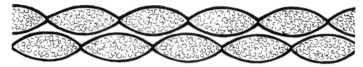

OVERLAPPING QUILTING

BOX WALL

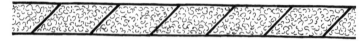

SLANT WALL

FIGURE 5

a good maker's name will, or should, mean that the design is good for the intended use of the bag.

PACKING AND STORING

Fibre-filled bags are usually made on the double-garment principle because of the way the material is quilted before it is cut into the shape of the bag. To get any thickness of insulation, two layers are required, and the result is a double bag. Regardless of cut or filling, the best way to pack a sleeping bag is to take it by the foot and stuff it into a stuff sack in handfuls, feeding the bag in until the drawstring of the stuffsack can be tightened. It does no good to a bag to be rolled, and for maximum longevity the bag should be hung straight when not in use. If you do not have room in your cupboard for this, the bag should be put away loosely folded in a large plastic storage bag where dust cannot get into it. A few mothballs will keep out prospective tenants.

CLEANING

The cleaning of dirty sleeping bags is simple in the case of man-made fibre bags and harder in the case of down. Fibre bags can be washed in a machine with no harm ensuing, but down cannot. Wash a down bag in the bath, with pure soap flakes, not detergent which will rob the down plumules of their essential oils. Rinse the bag very thoroughly, treading the water out with the feet over and over till it rinses the same colour as it goes in. Tread out all the surplus water before picking up the bag VERY CAREFULLY ALL ALONG ITS LENGTH. Careless handling at this stage can result in the soggy, heavy down cascading through the thin baffles to collect at the foot; your bag is then, to all intents, ruined. Dry the damp bag very carefully in natural heat for several days, frequently massaging the down lumps back into individual plumules. With care, a bag washed in this manner will regain its former loft and smell a lot sweeter.

Simple precautions in the use of sleeping bags include keeping them well away from naked flames and sparks which can ruin the nylon. The draw-cord around the hood should be threaded through a draw-string clamp, the ends being left as single strings rather than a loop in which you can catch your head. Should the bag be affected by condensation within the tent, dry it in the sun or air at the first opportunity, and always dry the bag thoroughly on return home. Do not store a damp bag; the down will start to rot, and the smell will keep you awake. Down is not allergenic or toxic in any way, but some people may react badly to the dust that static can attract to the nylon covering. If this is the case, try a cotton lined bag or a fibre-filled one. Many people like to put a linen lining inside their sleeping bag to keep it clean. I am not one of these; the lining tends to twist round the restless sleeper like a straightjacket. I prefer to use a suit of long underwear or a fibre-pile suit as sleeping wear. This will keep the bag as clean as any liner, without the hassle of tangling, and I can get out of bed in the night and still remain warm.

GROUND INSULATION

Even the finest of sleeping bag filling will be compressed under the body weight of the sleeper, and will give no insulation value in the compressed areas. For this reason, the backpacker should insulate himself from the cold of the earth by means of a closed-cell foam mat. Such mats are incredibly light, non-absorbent, and virtually indestructible except by fire; being plastic foam, once alight they melt and drip. They come in various lengths, from shoulders-to-hip, up to full length for winter use. I always carry at least the short one, padding the ground with my walking trousers under my knees and feet.

An alternative to the closed cell mat is an open cell one, giving much more comfort. It does absorb water however, and needs to be dried out regularly. If covered with a breathable but water repellant cover, on a totally waterproof base, it makes the best mattress for a comfort-loving backpacker and possesses more warmth than a light air-mattress. Air-beds tend to be heavy, and cold in use unless closed cell foam is placed under the sleeping bag on top of the air mattress. Air mattresses have the uncanny knack of letting you down with a puncture in the small hours of the morning, and in my estimation are more trouble than they are worth.

Other forms of ground insulation are thinner pieces of closed-cell foam, and layered plastic blankets of the type called "space-blankets" or "sportsmens' blankets". These are fine for use in the summer, but perform better the task of keeping heather stubs and small stones from puncturing the thin groundsheet of the tent than actually stopping more than a modicum of ground cold. They are more easily packed into a pack than the closed-cell mats or sleeping pads, and I rely on them in the warm summer months.

TENTS

The beginner, or the summer backpacker can probably get away without any shelter at all, provided that he chooses his weather forecast with care. Minimum shelter should be a sheet of plastic, for lightness, to keep the rain from wetting the sleeping bag. Large sheets of polythene can be bought at garden stores, and one of these, suspended from a nylon cord between two uprights will perform satisfactorily as a first tent.

The early morning rising, usually in the rain, will be the impetus that persuades a backpacker to buy a tent. A good tent can provide the sleeper with a 10 to 15 degree differential between the inside and the outside temperatures, allowing a light sleeping bag to be used for an extended season camping. The additional general comfort and shelter provided by a good tent is well worth the extra weight. For backpackers, tents in proofed nylon offer the best options.

Tents for the backpacker can be either single-skinned or double-skinned. A single-skinned proofed nylon tent is totally waterproof

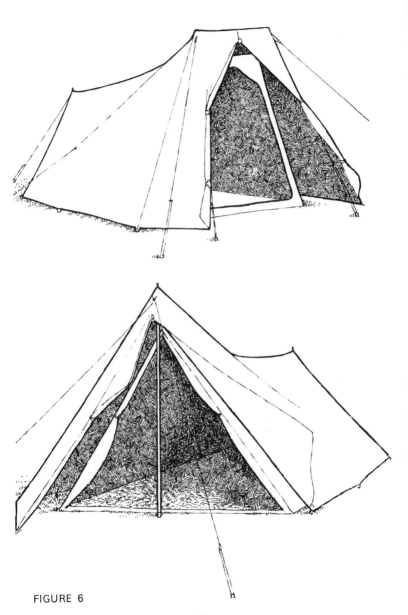

FIGURE 6

and provides the minimum weight shelter with all-round protection from weather and wind. These tents are superb in dry, or frosty weather, but unless very well ventilated by through drafts are as unpleasant to sleep in during condensation-type conditions, such as cool, damp nights, as an old Wellington boot. The walls will drip with the condensing body moisture of the sleeper, and the sleeping bag will soon be sodden by contact with the running walls. If the single skin tent is large enough however, the occupant can avoid touching the sides of the tent, but then the extra weight of the structure begins to intrude on the load carried.

Double-skinned tents have the outer tent, or flysheet, as totally waterproof as that of the single-skinned type. They differ though in that the double-skinned tent has a *breathable* inner tent suspended from the poles in a way that allows the occupant to remain separated from the condensation should it build up on the inside of the flysheet. The inner tent will have a sewn-in groundsheet providing a dry, insect-free cave for sleeping, while the best type of flysheet will be all enveloping, coming to the ground all round the tent. Rubber loop guylines will ensure adequate ventilation, and additional rings where the rubbers are attached will let you double peg the flysheet to the ground in case of high winds.

FLYSHEET AND INNER

The sort of separation you should look for between the inner and the outer tent will be about 10 cm. The larger the space between the two, the better the insulation will be. The best designs of tent for this country have archway entrances that allow free access to the inside without centre poles or guylines getting in the way, but which have a large sheltered storage space in the front or round the side of the tent where boots and packs can be placed out of the way, but still in the dry. Such tents are designed to be pitched tail into wind, and the tail is generally lower than the front where the occupant goes in and out. You sleep with your head near the door, and unless the weather is *very* cold or windy, I usually leave most of the door open. The zipper that shuts the door should allow you to have ventilation without rain striking in on you directly when you are asleep.

WEIGHT

As a general rule, you should not carry more than 4 lbs of tent, including pegs and poles, per person. The lone traveller can find double-skinned tents weighing less than this, which pack into very small bags. Two-person teams can save weight by doubling up on tentage. A good two-person tent can weigh between 5 and $6\frac{1}{2}$ lbs, giving each member of the team $2\frac{1}{2}$ to $3\frac{1}{4}$ lbs tentage each. Poles will be made of aluminium, and the best ones nest inside each other. Pegs should be aluminium, and can either be simple skewer-type, or V-angled aluminium. I do not like the plastic pegs except for boggy ground, as they are hard to clean and tend to snap if pushed into hard earth.

MATERIALS

Tent materials are now nearly all nylon, for maximum lightness and long life. Even the inner tent will be breathable uncoated nylon, though cotton inners can be found if nylon does not appeal. The days of the all-cotton tent are gone as far as the lightweight enthusiast is concerned. Cotton absorbs and holds moisture, making it heavy to carry when wet, and it rots if not carefully dried. Nylon is stronger, needs little drying, and is proofed.

BUYING A TENT

A backpacker's tent of any quality should be sought and bought from a specialist shop, not from the supermarket or Saturday bargain advertisements. It should be made by a reputable maker and should be made of polyurethane-proofed nylon. The inner tent should be breathable, either cotton or nylon, and the doors should close by coil zippers. All the seams should be properly finished off, and tape should preferably be stitched all round the base of the flysheet to spread the strain of a sudden gust of wind. There should be adequate means of holding the doors open so that the end of the door panel cannot blow round in a gust and knock the cooking pot off the stove. The front of the tent should be tall enough for a grown person to sit upright, and the length of the inner must allow a tall person in a sleeping bag room to stretch out flat. The inner should be roomy enough so that the occupant or occupants may have enough elbow room without being forced into the sides of the tent.

The construction of the tent should be neat in appearance, with all the sewing neatly done, and having 8 or 9 stitches to the inch. There should be proper reinforcement where the poles fit, and all guying points must be strong enough to take extra guys in case of high winds. Poles and pegs must be sufficient in number when you check the tent over before delivery, and must obviously fit together easily. A good design of tent will allow you to pitch the flysheet first in foul weather, so that all further unpacking may be done under shelter. There ought to be full protection or a porch for the occupants in the mouth of the tent, where the backpacker does a lot of living and cooking. There should be room enough for all the backpacker's gear inside or by the flysheet, under cover.

Depending on the sort of backpacking you are intending to do, you should choose between a tent to give you maximum space for living in, and one that is the very lightest structure you can carry, consistent with wind-resistance. The camper who walks should go for space, while the walker who camps will spend less time under cover, letting him carry a lighter, more compact tent. Do not be in too much hurry to buy a good tent; think your own problems through first.

Chapter 3

COOKING

The conservation-minded backpacker no longer cooks on an open fire. The reasons range from the mere fact that there are now so many of us backpacking that fuel would present a sizeable problem in a short space of time, to the sheer inconvenience of firelighting. In order to cook meals where and when he likes, the backpacker can choose from a wide range of small, light, compact stoves designed for his specific purposes.

FUELS

Fuel types begin with solid blocks of hexamine and other combustible substances, which while good enough for boiling the odd cup of tea, are not sufficient as a regular heat source for cooking main meals. Better by far are liquid fuels, such as Petrol, Paraffin and Methylated Spirits. Of these, the most efficient year-round burners and providers of great heat, in a controllable form, are petrol and paraffin. Petrol is easy to come by, although the small quantities needed by the backpacker may make a pump attendant snort. For this reason, as well as for filling the stove tank, it is wise to carry a very small plastic funnel. Paraffin is an old favourite among the older campers, but does not seem to be so popular today as beginners object to the smell of the fuel if spilt, and to the need to carry another type of priming fuel for pre-heating the burner plate. Paraffin remains the cheapest form of fuel though.

Methylated spirits is a relatively safe form of fuel which does not have to burn in a pressure tank to provide heat. You have only to pour out the spirit into the burner cup and light it, and the stove is ready for use. It burns silently, and in the right stove is almost windproof. The only disadvantages are that most meths stoves are thirsty, burning a lot of fuel which must therefore be carried in quantity for any period longer than a weekend.

Containers for all liquid fuels should ideally be metal, with screw-top lids that seal effectively Paraffin and meths may be carried quite satisfactorily in plastic bottles providing that the lid can be made secure, but even so I would wrap the bottle in a plastic bag or two for safety, and to avoid contamination of food. When it comes to the carriage of petrol, containers of greater integrity are needed. They should be made of metal, with a tightly fitting screw-top that has a petrol-proof washer between the bottle and the cap. The best bottles are made on the Continent, but an acceptable substitute is a hydraulic fluid container that holds about $\frac{1}{3}$-pint. Garages use a lot of brake fluid, and you should be able to get a couple of these tins from a garage without charge.

Another easily carried fuel is butane gas. This is available for a large range of small stoves, and can be obtained in either screw-top canisters or pierceable cartridges. Butane is a liquid which gasifies under pressure, and the canisters are pressurised, forcing the liquid into the burner through a jet; the resulting gas is burned like that in a normal household cooker. The one trouble with butane is that in cold conditions it will not gasify, and the liquid will only flare dangerously, giving off little heat. There are two alternatives when the weather is too cold for the butane to operate efficiently. One is to use a stove designed to burn liquid butane by means of a preheating tube in the fuel circuit, and the other is to warm the gas canister by body heat prior to lighting the stove.

Propane which will gasify below zero, is not at present available in small containers.

STOVES

So much for the types of fuel. The stoves to use with each type range from the simple, in the case of the solid fuel, to the ultra-sophisticated in the case of the winter gas stove. In between lie the paraffin pressure stove, the same design that has been around for a good many years and is therefore tried and tested, and the petrol stoves of which the same can be said. The meths stoves that I know and trust are of two separate types—the Turmsport, which has a tank of fuel and the ability to simmer by means of a control tap, and the Trangia. This last is a truly wind-proof, simple, stable and efficient burner that comprises a burner stand with a built-in windscreen-cum-potholder, and a set of top-range cooking pots. The pots are placed into the windscreen, where the heat of the burner literally wraps all around them, using the maximum heating surface available. If the frying pan lid is inverted over the pot, this assists in heat retention, and speeds up the boiling of the pot. One of the best things about the Trangia is that it burns silently, so that you can hear when the water begins to bubble. (Figure 7)

Pressure stoves burn paraffin or petrol. The first must be primed with either methylated spirits or solid fuel, and has to be lit by a more complicated method than I now like to be bothered with. Priming fuel is placed round the burner tube, the screw in the

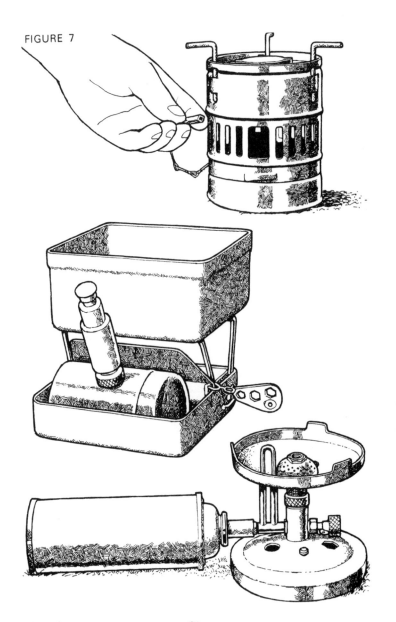

FIGURE 7

top of the filler cap is loosened off to release any air pressure in the tank, and the priming is lit. When it is almost burnt out, you tighten the screw in the filler cap and pump the built-in pressure pump forcing the paraffin up the warmed-up tube in a spray of vapourised fuel. This should be ignited by the last flames of the priming fuel. To increase the heat of the flame, pump more air into the tank. To shut off the stove, open the screw on the filler cap.

It is simpler with the petrol pressure-stoves. With the SVEA 123, the lightest and simplest of them all, you only have to open the fuel tap on the burner stem and hold a lighter or a match under the tank. This will cause a fine jet of petrol to rise up the tube and spray against the burner plate, running down into a recess in the top of the tank. When this trough is partly full of petrol, turn off the fuel tap, place the stove on a flat, hard surface and light the fuel in the trough. A tall, yellow flame will envelope the top of the stove; it is advisable NOT to do this within the confines of a small nylon tent, as the flame will at best melt the material, and at worst kill you with carbon monoxide poisoning if it is left burning in a badly-ventilated area. Always beware of cooking fumes and flame when in the tent.

When the fuel has nearly burnt away, open the fuel tap again with the key, and the stove will roar into life, burning with a rather noisy blue flame. Do not open the tap as far as it will open, as the stove will then be burning at maximum heat, which may cause pressure to build up too much inside the tank. Keep the heat level down by means of the tap to the exact degree of heat required. To extinguish the flame, turn off the fuel tap with the key provided. To avoid the key becoming very hot to the touch, take it off the stove while the cooking is going on.

While the SVEA 123 is the smallest and lightest stove burning petrol, a somewhat more stable version is the Optimus 99. This sits lower on the ground, and has a small, square cooking pot that doubles as a lid for the stove. For a two-person party, I recommend this stove because of its added stability with bigger pots; also, when two people are in a small tent, there is an increased likelihood of someone moving about, and possibly knocking a cooking pot and stove over.

Butane gas stoves are the simplest and most convenient type for the beginner. There is usually a tap on the stove to control the fuel flow and by closing this off, the stove can be shut down. Real simmering heat can be easily obtained, and the stove can be instantly relit at the touch of a match or a lighter. Relighting pro-

34

cedures on a pressurised stove, are by comparison with gas more lengthy and can be dangerous if not carried out according to the instructions that come with the stove.

The winter-gas stove mentioned briefly above is a winter gas-burner that has a pre-heater tube through which the butane liquid flows. The canister of gas fits sideways onto the stove, which is lit by standing it upright so as to use the small pocket of residual gas that stays in the top of the canister *despite* the low temperature. Once the gas is lit, the pre-heater tube warms up and the liquid butane flowing through is instantly gasified to burn as normal. Both this and the summer version can be folded into itself like an oyster to provide the backpacker with the smallest possible effective stove.

COOKING POTS

Probably the cheapest form of long-lasting cooking pots for the beginner are the standard issue Army mess-tins that can still be bought at surplus shops. They are heavy and bulky though, and do not compare with a properly designed set of pans for the solo camper. The basic requirements for one person in the cooking equipment field are at least one pot of about $1\frac{1}{2}$ pint capacity, together with a frying-pan lid. Such an outfit is limiting however in the number of variations that can be discovered in terms of one's own style of cookery, and a better set would have at least two pans and a lid together with a large plastic mug.

A set like this can be used to prepare a fair-sized meal without having to clean pans between courses. A set like this can be extended to cover the needs of a party of three or so by the addition of a real frying-pan, and the use of an extra, larger pot in which to boil more than $1\frac{1}{2}$ pints of water at a time. Nowadays, really good, lightweight 2-pint pans are hard to come by, and if water-boiling is the aim, I suggest that a large cake-tin makes an excellent substitute for a ready-made expensive pan.

Backpackers' cooking pots should be simple in design, but should be strong as well as light. Often they will serve as containers for fragile things such as eggs, and thin pans are easily crushed. Thin pans also allow food to burn, especially when placed over small, intense heat sources such as petrol stoves. There should be no ridges around the inside or the outside to catch stray bits of food or to impede swift washing-up. The rims should be fully rolled over to prevent catching food in them, and also to allow a pan-holder to be used without cutting into the metal of the pan. Large flat pans should be avoided as they can spill reflected heat onto the fuel tank thereby raising the temperature inside the tank to a dangerous level! The pressure valve will then blow out, creating a hazard to the cook and others in the vicinity.

A compromise must be reached between capacity and height of the pans. A flat pan is easier to fit into a pack while a deep pan is more efficient when used on a small, powerful heat source; the food cooks all the way through in a taller pot than in a flat one with a central heat spot and cooler edges. Rather than have every pot fitted with its own handle, a separate pot-grab is a good contribution to the overall lightness of the set.

SUNDRIES

A large plastic drinking mug is better than a small one as it takes less fuel to make a large brew than it does for two small ones. A 1-pint mug can be marked inside and out as a measuring cup for indicating the correct amounts of water needed to reconstitute dried food. If a frying-pan is carried, it should be a non-stick one to ease the washing-up burden, and it should have its own non-stick spatula for turning over the food. Forks are not needed by backpackers, generally speaking, as a spoon will serve to eat any sort of simple meals that a packer is likely to prepare. If a knife is needed, the pocket knife can be used to cut food into bite-sized chunks which are then eaten with a spoon. A luxury I permit myself is an extra, smaller spoon for tea-brewing, as I never seem to have a clean spoon otherwise when it comes to putting the milk and sugar into my mug.

Chapter 4

FOOD

Food, as always, is a matter of personal likes and dislikes. The aim is to combine palatability with portability, and attempts to marry the two have not been inevitably successful. The choices open to the backpacker are to take fresh food, tinned food or Accelerated Freeze-Dried food (AFD). Fresh will do for the first day or so in cooler weather, but retains its moisture content and is therefore heavy. Tins possess most of their moisture plus the weight of the tin and are thus very heavy indeed; they may however contain pre-cooked food which only requires to be heated-up to eat, unlike fresh food. The fuel saving on such a meal may balance out the extra weight of the tin.

DEHYDRATED FOODS

Lightest by far is dehydrated food such as AFD. With these, all the moisture in the ingredients has been sucked out, and must be replaced by the backpacker when he needs the meal. Cooking times for these meals are based on the time needed not only to cook the mixture, but to reconstitute the moisture content prior to cooking. until recently, preparation times for such meals have included simmering for as long as 25 minutes after bringing to the boil! Such procedure fills a small tent with steam and condensation besides frustrating the hungry backpacker who is usually ravenous enough to eat the meal rather underdone. Much can be done to cut the simmering time by pre-soaking the meal for the evening in a polythene bottle while you walk along in the afternoon. By the time you set up camp, the majority of the meal will be ready for straight cooking, and simmering time may be cut by half.

A new type of recently introduced AFD food has cut the preparation down even more, so that all you do is add the right amount of water, boil, simmer for five minutes and then eat. This is only one step away from the American method of pouring the right amount of boiling water into the food bag, letting it stand and mix for five minutes, and then eating direct from the bag. This is an even greater fuel-saving method than pre-soaking.

The majority of AFD meals contain meat substitute (textured soya protein) rather than actual dried meat, which is available, though very expensive. As in all things, there are various qualities of this meat substitute, and you will know when you have eaten a cheaper version by the lingering, rather metallic taste. The beginner is well advised to try every meal on the market before deciding which suits his individual palate, but at the same time, it is worth remembering that specialist foods designed for the camper and walker are, by very reason of their limited market, over-priced compared with food that can be obtained from groceries and supermarkets.

SHOPPING

From these sources can be bought fast-cooking vegetables, rice, macaroni and other cereals that can make many an appetising meal. Many backpackers use Muesli, the Swiss breakfast food as a staple of their diet, especially when the basic Muesli mixture is either concocted at home from ingredients bought at a health store, or is the supermarket version with one's own additions such as Horlicks powder, brown sugar, grated chocolate, raisins and currants. The great thing about Muesli is that it requires little preparation in the morning, and can be eaten with either hot or cold water poured over the top in lieu of milk. Dried milk powder mixed in beforehand helps to make the taste better, and the effect of 4 oz of the stuff seems to last until lunchtime without the walker suffering from "hunger bonk", which strikes without warning and leaves one feeling rather washed-out and un-eager to proceed further.

Lunch dishes can include packet soups, crackers or Ryvita-type biscuits, with cheese, fruit, salami or smoked sausage, or even sandwiches brought from home. Whatever you eat should replace the energy lost during the morning, and the beginner should aim off a bit for an appetite larger than his normal one. In backpacking circles lunch begins shortly after breakfast and goes on through the day until tea-time, which then continues till dinner is prepared. A constant dribble of easy-to-reach trail-food is better for the digestion than a great wad of a meal at a set time into an empty stomach.

Most books on backpacking seem to provide a long table of calorie and protein requirements per day under conditions of heavy toil. The average British backpacker, in my experience, seems only to go out for relatively short periods, such as weekends, and can probably afford to eat as much or as little as he likes without suffering from scurvy or the like. In summer, my appetite drops in the heat, and rises like a hawk in the winter. It is generally a good idea however to get into the habit of planning for and carrying an extra main meal in case you get caught out overnight when you did not expect it. You may consistently bring the extra meal home, but sooner or later you will find a use for it. If you go into the hills you will need emergency rations anyway.

DRINKS

As far as beverages go, I have settled on tea as being the staple one I carry. For some reason, it tastes cleaner on the tongue when I am walking, and I have found that my normal brew of coffee tends to cloy a bit. Tea for the solo packer is most conveniently made from teabags, and I allow about fifteen bags for a long weekend; invariably I bring some back again. In the winter I add a small container of cocoa to the pack, for a last hot drink before going to sleep. I eat a small bit of chocolate at the same time, and the calories seem to fuel the furnace for a warm night's rest. Although all the authorities agree that alcohol should not be taken in cold weather, I still retain a liking for a drink in the evening, and carry a small flask; this again is symptomatic of backpacking, which is, above all things, a truly individual pastime as far as choice of personal equipment is concerned.

So my last word on food would be that if you happen to like fish-fingers fried in jam, then take it with you and do not be put off by the likes of others. In terms of fuel carried, I tend to use small tins of food rather than fresh or AFD, but AFD certainly cuts the day's load if you can be sure of getting plenty of water at cooking time. Unless you are a great chef, I suggest that there are better ways of passing the time when backpacking than slaving over a hot stove. Make your food tasty but convenient.

Chapter 5

ACCESSORIES

Although the walking camper should keep his kit to a minimum, there are certain accessory items that add versatility to a pack and enjoyment to a trip. The most obvious one is a First Aid kit and I will deal with that and its contents later.

Having glossed over that item, I shall also gloss over the Compass, except to say that this accessory should be taken on every trip in the country, as a habit; it should be used also as a habit, to accustom the user to every technique of compasswork so that he is prepared if any emergency should arise. You also need the appropriate map or maps. The best way to start learning the correct use of map and compass is to read a good basic book, such as "The Spurbook of Map and Compass". The subject deserves a book to itself, and every beginning backpacker should have this one in his library.

FIGURE 8

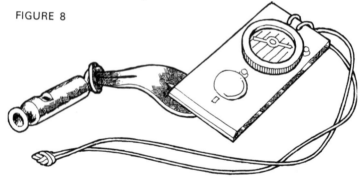

Carried together with the compass is a Whistle, for attracting attention and for signalling over distances. Mine is orange, to help in finding it if it falls in the grass. The distress signal with a whistle is six short blasts, followed by a minute's silence, then repeated continuously. (Figure 8)

Knives are a very personal item. The backpacker's real needs are met by a simple penknife with a blade no longer than an inch or so, but I own many knives (I once collected them) and still cannot force myself to do without something a bit bigger and more complicated than the basic small bladed penknife. I cannot rationally carry a long-bladed sheathknife any more, and find that a lock-back knife that folds is just as good. But I know full well I do not need it.

A lighter is useful for conveniently lighting the stove, whatever its type. My lighter is a small gas cylinder with a variable flame that can be shot into the priming cup of my petrol stove. I still carry Matches as well, both the windproof sort and normal safety matches, as there have been times when the lighter did not work. Matches by themselves would really be enough.

The best sort of Tinopener is the "Baby" folding-bladed kind, as issued in the Army. It weighs $\frac{1}{2}$ oz, and needs a bit of string tying to it to keep it visible, on the grass or ground. (Figure 9)

FIGURE 9

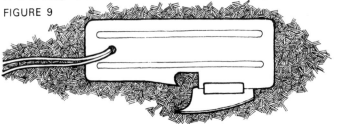

The Washing-up kit can be very small. A small scouring pad removes those errors of cooking that cake onto the pots, and a couple of J-cloths will do all the mopping and drying required. A small container of detergent washing powder can be useful. Luxury is a separate tea-towel for real drying-up. Personal kit for me consists of a folding toothbrush, some bio-degradable soap in a tube, some toothpaste in a cut-off tube, a comb, some lipsalve, some Optone eye drops in case of dust or tiredness after a day in the wind, some paper handkerchiefs, toilet paper, some antiseptic cream and a spare packet of indigestion tablets.

Water is a necessity, and must either be carried or collected on arrival. In either case, a container is essential. The simplest bottle is a plastic one that comes from the supermarket with squash inside. Many different types are available, but the capacity should not be less than a litre unless several are carried. I find that I need about a gallon a day in all, for my needs between stopping for the night, and starting out again the next morning. That includes a freeze-dried meal, and at least three brews of tea, plus a good wash. There are excellent folding bottles that hold this much, and weigh about 4 oz. If the only water looks a bit dirty, it makes sense to drop some chlorine tablets in; these can be got from a chemist, or backpacking shop.

Lighting can be either a small torch, with spare batteries, or a candle. The torch should be fitted with long-life Mallorycells, and the AA size is quite adequate. Once you are inside the tent, and more or less stationary, the candle can be lit and placed in a cooking pot for safety. Keep it away from the material of the tent, or the tent will burn down round you. A candle produces surprising amounts of heat in a small tent, and the light is enough to read by.

If you plan on keeping a journal, a pen and writing paper are needed. I have good resolutions about this, but usually manage to leave the paper behind. A paperback book is a great comfort if you know that you will have some time to spare, such as in the long winter nights. Otherwise, the map you will be carrying in a plastic bag, or even a proper Map Case, will prove pretty rivetting reading.

An alternative source of entertainment could well be a Radio. One of the reasons I go backpacking, however, is to get away from all that sort of thing, and although I have got a very tiny radio which works on the same kind of batteries as the torch, I generally leave it behind. When I do take it I use a miniature earphone with it to avoid disturbing other people.

Binoculars are a boon for finding the path or looking at the local wild life. I have managed to reduce my requirements to a pocket-sized monocular weighing a few ounces; they are nice to have, but once again, they are not really necessary unless birdwatching is what you go backpacking for.

The backpacker's Camera is worthy of a book to itself, I suppose. I have carried just about everything from single-lens reflexes to tiny sub-miniatures, and now rely largely on a very small full-frame 35 mm camera that lives in a pouch on my belt. And for most of the time, that is exactly where it stays. I am finding now that it is more worthwhile developing The Camera Of The Mind, and bring back back memories rather than negatives. Together with all the heavy gear I have ditched the extra lenses, flash units, tripods and filters that used to inhabit my daily world. If you are a real camera freak though, nothing I can say will change your mind about what you carry, and if you are NOT a camera freak, you don't have that problem to worry about.

Boots get very scuffed in the heather and long grass and I take a small pot of dressing in a plastic bag together with a bit of cloth; I rub some of the dressing into my boots in the evening.

Chapter 6

CARRYING THE LOAD

The human body is capable of carrying some fairly substantial loads, especially if they are carried correctly, high and close to the spine. A well-designed backpack is the most efficient and comfortable way of carrying all the equipment that a walking camper requires to keep him warm and safe under all weather conditions. By using modern pack technology, the carrying of equipment now becomes a matter of personal selection of features, rather than a choice of carrying method.

The most basic backpack is simply a bag, with straps to fasten over the hiker's shoulders. The load is put in from the top, and tends to sag against the wearer's back, pulling him over backwards. To counterbalance such an action, the walker must use musclepower to lean forward, and thus becomes more tired than he would be if he were able to walk upright.

The strongest weight-bearing part of the body is the pelvis, and weight can be absorbed there more readily than on the shoulders. By means of a padded hip belt, the pack weight may be transferred to the pelvic region, allowing the shoulder straps to hold the pack against the back rather than carry the whole load. With the load carried by the pelvis, the walker can stride along in a more comfortable stance. Most of the packs used by backpackers take this hip-belt principle as a standard feature, and only loads of *less than 15 lbs* should be carried without a hipbelt.

The belt is fastened to the base of the pack. It should be padded, as it must be tightened round the hips in order to fulfil its weight-bearing function, and might cut into the flesh if made too thin. Most of today's padded hip-belts have some sort of quick-release buckle, which lets the wearer shed the pack fast in case of emergency, such as if he were to slip while crossing a stream.

Modern packs can be either made with a padded back, for the maximum comfort and lightness, or they can be constructed to fit onto a frame. The high-frame pack is a very fine way to carry a really heavy load, but for the average weekend backpacker the best choice remains the frameless pack if it is fitted with the hip-belt.

FIGURE 10

MATERIALS

Packs may be made out of either cotton duck or nylon that has been proofed with polyurethane. Cotton duck is heavier, but less susceptible to scuffing; nylon is lighter and possibly more waterproof. It will always be a personal choice, as there are some people who do not care for the feel of nylon. The average backpacker looks for lightness, however, and nylon is the obvious choice.

If the packload for a weekend's backpacking is not more than 25 lbs, or the walker is carrying only light summer gear, a frameless pack allows the extra weight of the frame to be dispensed with. The frameless pack is generally made somewhat smaller, thus encouraging the backpacker to keep his load to a minimum. Packbags made to fit onto a frame are quite voluminous, to carry winter loads, and tempt the beginner into carrying something extra "just because there is still room in the pack". My own choice leans heavily towards the frameless, or "soft" pack nowadays, and I can get a week's load of food, fuel and gear into my favourite bag with ease. I have not carried a frame for at least a year now.

FRAMES

When the pack load begins to climb towards the 40 lb mark, a frame will definitely assist the wearer to carry the weight near to the spine, and as high on the shoulders as can be managed. Modern frames are made of alloy tubing, with cross-bars that may be welded or screwed into the uprights. The uprights themselves are shaped to the back in a mild S-bend, and a completely straight upright tube should be avoided. The hip-belt is fastened at the base of the frame, and another backband bears the pack weight across the wearer's back below the shoulder blades. This backband may be made of mesh in an attempt to ventilate the bearing surface. More usual backbands are broad nylon bands that are tightened by cords or even metal turnbuckles.

The problems of sweating under the pressure of a backband or a frameless pack depends for a solution on the individual and his metabolism. My own experience has been that I can sweat just as much under a full-mesh backband as I do against a "soft" pack with a fully-padded canvas back; the extra ventilation appears not to work for me. This loads the odds in favour of the lighter pack, as far as I am concerned. In theory though, there *should* be a far greater flow of cooling air between the back and the frame pack than there is with a soft pack that gains a great deal of extra

FIGURE 11

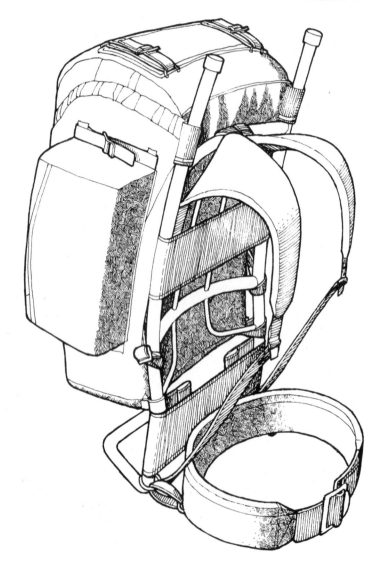

purchase and stability by pressing against a larger surface of the wearer's back.

There is no reason why the harness of either type of pack should differ greatly. The shoulder straps should be well padded, and preferably should taper towards the lower fastening so as to avoid cutting into the tender area of the armpit. They should be broad where they pass over the shoulders, and at this point they should be horizontal to, or slightly sloping up to, the attachment point on the frame or pack. Any curving over he shoulders down to the attachment point indicates that the harness is too small; the pack will tend to lean backwards off the wearer, causing extra effort in walking. The straps may fasten to the frame with loops, pins or buckles. The best way is to have them fastened to the frame with a strap and buckle, as pins and rings tend to squeak and rattle. At the base of the frame, the same fastenings will be found, and may combine with the lower fixing of the hip-belt.

The aim of the harness is to hold the whole pack against the back of the walker. The bag that goes on the frame, or forms the body of the "soft" pack may come in a bewildering variety of shapes, sizes, colours and features. The capacity is generally measured in litres, which conveys little to the beginner until he sees a bag beginning to absorb his own particular gear. The tendency is to "over-bag" for the individual's requirement on the grounds that one may want to go on a long trip. I think it more logical to assess one's backpacking in terms of the number of weekends to be spent in the outdoors and plan the pack load for this requirement, while allowing for expansion of the load by means of add-on stuffsacks for the occasional longer trip. This not only solves the main problem, that of the many weekends spent carrying a light load, but is a cheaper first solution to the whole pack problem. Subsequent experience may well indicate another, larger pack, but the smaller one will always be useful as a summer pack, and one should grow into the bigger one in time.

PACK FEATURES

Pockets are a very useful feature on a packsack. They allow small items to be located quickly and easily without disturbing the main load, and a method of packing can be arranged so that everything has its own habitual place. Pockets let the weight distribution be more even, as do partitions inside the main compartment. One of the commonest of these is to make a partition to divide the main sack into a top and a bottom section. In summer, a light load can be carried in the top section and pockets only, with room to expand the winter kit into the lower space. Most compartments such as this have the inner corners cut out to allow tent poles in their bags to be pushed down inside the pack, using the full height. Some even have a zipper around the inside, to allow the bag to be used as one big space instead of two smaller ones.

Packs to fit frames can either be made to fill the whole frame space, or else to take only two-thirds of the frame. The latter let the backpacker tie additional equipment such as the closed-cell foam pad, or even the sleeping bag, under the main pack against the base of the frame, usually in a separate stuffsack. Another stuff sack may even be carried on the top of the pack, and to cope with such elongated loads it is possible to buy an extender bar for the frame. These are specialist expedition frames though, and do not feature regularly as part of the British scene unless the backpacker is carrying everything including the kitchen sink.

Despite the polyurethane coating of the pack material, no pack can be said to be truly waterproof. All contents that are liable to get wet should always be double-wrapped in plastic bags, and possibly in thin stuff-sacks for maximum protection. If the owner of the pack has the patience, the stitchholes of the seams may be doped by using Bostik No. 1, or Copydex. The best solution however is a pack cover; the cheapest is a dustbin-liner, with a hole cut in the back for the shoulder harness, which is then passed through the hole and re-fastened at the frame base.

The aim of the pack is to carry the items that comprise the backpacker's home, and to afford comfort while being carried. An ill-fitting pack is a menace, a well-fitting one a joy. It is worth spending a little time on the selection of a good pack, and it is worth spending more money to get the right one for you.

Chapter 7

PLANNING A TRIP

The whole idea of getting all this backpacking gear is to get out into the countryside and use it. Perhaps you have started with the aim of immediately doing one of the Long-distance Footpaths that cover the country like the motorway network. My advice at this stage would be—DON'T.

The first trip should be made nearer to home, with the intention of getting you used to everything you have acquired, from your boots to your new diet. It will take time to adjust yourself to such things as getting a good night's rest in the solitude of your little tent, surrounded by strange night noises.

Good memories come from good trips, and good trips begin with good planning. The planning of any venture is really a part of the total pleasure, as the anticipation is just the first stage of a three-part experience; anticipation, performance and finally, memory. So far, we have gone through the stage of assembling a basic kit and now come to the selection of an area in which to use it. The first few days in your backpacking life should be spent near home, if you are fortunate enough to live in the country. If not, then choose a bit of country near to a quick route back to your home. This is only to give you the confidence that if anything awkward should happen, you are not entirely at the mercy of the elements.

FIRST TRIP

The simplest trip is just an "overnight". This, in summer, involves the most basic kit of all; your tent may be a piece of plastic sheeting spread overhead on a line, and you can exist easily without a stove. Your food will be cold things brought out from home, and there is nothing wrong with water for drinking. Your sleeping bag and closed-cell mat will give you a comfortable night's rest, and a sweater and the raingear will be all that's needed to complete your first rudimentary pack. The aim is to walk somewhere, carrying your overnight gear, and to enjoy yourself. This first day's walk, and overnight camp, will show you some of the pleasures of backpacking, and probably some areas in which your kit could be improved. But above all, it should fire you with ambition to do a real trip, as soon as you can.

FURTHER TRAINING

One overnight walk does not make you a backpacker, but you will be well on the way, simply by acknowledging that you enjoy such an experience and wish to do it again. So plan another trip, a bit further afield, leaving yourself an "escape" route if need be, but placing more emphasis on self-reliance, and trying all the time to do something not previously attempted. Have an Aim for the trip. Perhaps you've always wanted to see a certain place, or monument; plan a trip and go and see it. One of the simplest exercise, if you're stuck for ideas, is to walk from one side of a given map sheet to the other. Picking the route will be good practice, and will help you to be able to recognise a good route from a bad one just by looking at the map, when you have done it a few times.

WEEKEND TRIPS

Let's assume though, that you have done the above, in easy stages, and you now know enough about the workings of your own kit to do a three-day weekend somewhere. My own routine would look something like this:

Having acquired a map of the area, I would look for a route that in all likelihood would give me a circular route, over varied country, to bring me back to the transport that brought me to the startpoint. (In most of my planning, I rely on my car to get me there and back, but it is just as simple with public transport, and at least then you can do a linear walk, from A to B, rather than returning to A). As I shall need a little time to shake down on the journey, I will plan a fairly short walk for the first day, over easy terrain, and will reckon to find a site in the late afternoon so as to pitch in a leisurely manner. The next day will be harder, and I would try to head for higher ground; I like hills, and they tend to be less inhabited than the flat bits. Pitching the second night on the hills would be my intention, with a third night spent as high as possible, returning to the car the morning of the fourth day.

I would try to find out as much as I could about the weather I'd be likely to find at the time of year of the trip, and would also try to do some reading about the local attractions. My best trips are to the places where our ancestors lived, and I particularly like looking for their fortified camps, in inaccessible spots. Having an aim in view turns the walk into an expedition instead of a saunter. So far, I know where I'm going, how I will get there and back, what conditions to expect, what I am looking for when I get there

50

and the sort of distances I will expect to make each day in order to achieve my aim and keep to my timetable.

One word about timetables; don't lose sight of the fact that a backpacker, because he carries his needs with him, is never forced into a rigid timetable. He can vary the object of his journey at the drop of a hat, and can even stop in one spot for the whole of the available time if that is what he suddenly decides. That is why backpacking is for the free spirits among us.

KIT CHECK
The next thing will be to make a list, assemble the gear, and ensure that it is clean and in good working order. I try never to use a new item without trying it out at home first, and this goes double for anything I want to eat. Any new recipe I always try to cook first under civilised conditions, but I always remember that all food tastes better if you eat it when you are hungry and tired; it helps to know that what you are going to cook and eat is easy to prepare on a small stove, and will taste good when it is done.

FOOD
I base my rations on a basis of muesli, 3 or 4 oz of it, suitably "stiffened" by my own extras, for breakfast, with a pint of tea. Lunch will be instant soup, probably the "cup of soup" size to avoid boiling up huge quantities of water on a limited fuel supply, more tea, and biscuits and cheese taken from a small plastic food box. Some trail snacks such as small chocolate bars, peanuts and raisins, apples or glucose sweets will be put in, enough for the number of days I'll be walking. Some sweet biscuits make tea-time another moveable feast, and the evening meal will probably be a small tin, a packet or even a piece of fresh meat the first night out. From the tin or packet though will come the main part of the meal; the purist may wonder why I bother with tins of food, and the reason is that food that has been already cooked saves fuel and cooking time. The weight of the tin equates with the weight of the fuel needed to cook something from scratch in most cases, and the shorter cooking times keep down the condensation in the tent.

All this food is bagged up in plastic bags, and the brew kit is overhauled. This consists of some little plastic tubes or boxes containing teabags, sugar and dried milk. Sometimes another little bottle of cocoa powder goes in too. All unnecessary packaging is removed, so that I am not carrying around extra rubbish to be carried home again. I pack another couple of plastic bags to put all the rubbish into, and what I pack into the trip area, I pack out again for proper disposal.

PACKING THE SACK
The kit is packed into the rucksack according to weight, and how often I will need to get at it. The first thing in is the closed-cell mat, rolled into the pack and allowed to unfurl. This then forms a tube down which the remainder of the gear is placed. Sleeping bag first, spare clothing next, main food bag, warm sweater and gloves, tent poles down the side of the pack, inner tent and fly-sheet with the pegs on top, waterproofs and the day's food all go into the main part of the sack. Outer pockets hold the stove and fuel, the cookset and brewkit, plus the spoons and washing-up kit. The waterbottle and first-aid kit, trail snacks and matches, and any other small items like the torch, all go into the smaller pockets, leaving the map to fit into the top of the pack, or to be tucked behind the frame if that's how you want to carry the gear.

CLOTHING
My own clothing will consist of a stringvest, a wool shirt, tweed trousers, two pairs of socks, and my boots which will have been cleaned and freshly treated with dressing. My knife will be on my belt, my money and identification in my pocket, my camera and film about my person, and my keys fit into a pouch on the hipbelt of the pack together with my monocular and my lighter. One more look through the checklist to see that nothing has been left undone, and I can put the pack into the car, lock the house, and hit the road. This is really where all the planning will pay off.

Chapter 8

ON THE TRAIL

There's an old Irish blessing that says "May the road rise before you, May the wind be always at your back". It's a good wish for the walker, because if the road is rising, the chances are that it will shortly drop too, and will provide a change of pace. As for the wind, take it from me that whichever way you go, it is generally blowing right in your face.

The carpark is now far behind. We've been climbing for some time now, and we are moving steadily towards the top of the first real ridge of the high country. The heather is starting to appear, and the ground is getting rather black with peat. Perhaps it seems a bit boggy underfoot, and this will be a good time to try out the knee-length gaiters that will keep the bits of heather, and the splash from the occasional puddle from getting into the socks and the top of the boots. As the wind rises, the air seems a bit cooler, even though it is summer, and as we top out onto the ridge itself, it is better described as chilly. Pause for a second, out with the rain jacket, and instantly the wind loses its bite. Walking for another mile or so brings the welcome warmth back to the body, but the hands are still cold. Pulling them up into the sleeves of the rain jacket will avoid having to pull on the gloves which are still deep in the pack. A sharp shower of rain may bring on the need to wear the trousers that go with the rain jacket, and you might want to pull the hood over your head, but soon the rain has gone, and the wind begins to drop.

When it starts to feel like a good time for lunch, look around for a quiet sheltered spot with a view of the countryside you have spent so much time and trouble to come to see. Put the loaded pack down carefully and if you haven't brought a short piece of closed-cell foam to sit on, try taking off your gaiters and allowing your legs to breathe again. Sitting on one gaiter, you can use the other to act as a tablecloth, on which all the food and implements can be laid out clear of the damp ground. Now you put the stove together, and put a pint of water on to boil. If the wind is still strong, put up some kind of windscreen, even your pack if necessary. While the water boils, get out the biscuits, and put the soup powder into your plastic mug or one of the smaller cooking pots, ready for the hot water. A tube of "squeeze cheese" and a tomato or two from home will build a tasty lunch with the soup, and a piece of chocolate or mintcake with the tea will round off the meal. A drop of cold water on a J-cloth will rinse the soup bowl, and later the tea mug, and the whole brewkit goes back into the pocket of the pack with the remains of lunch.

As you wander along getting back into your stride, you can begin to feel the concrete of the everyday life losing its hold on you. Just as you start to become aware of the feel of the country, perhaps another awareness begins to nag—there's a hot spot on your foot, signalling an incipient blister. Stop at once; the first-aid pack is needed, and you reach for the piece of "Moleskin" you brought for this purpose. Of course, you should have tried to break in the boots a bit more before going on a real hike like this, but no one is perfect, and you must learn sooner or later what a blister feels and looks like. On the heel of your foot is a small red patch, which feels tender. Taking a bit of moleskin, you cut a patch somewhat bigger than the painful area, and take the greatest care to round off the edges of the dressing. This so that the square corners do not cause the sock to catch and lift the moleskin dressing, causing it to bunch and stick to the sock. If your socks are damp with sweat, this is a good time to fetch another pair out of your pack, and change them. Blisters are caused by friction, heat and damp, and cool dry feet go a long way to preventing blisters.

Now you are looking around for a water source, as the air becomes cooler, and the sun begins to sink towards the horizon. A stream is ideal, but a cattle trough with clean water will do. I reckon that if there are things living in any pond, the water is clean enough to drink; not even insects will live in stagnant water. The pack will feel heavier with the water you are packing, but you can now stop anywhere for the night and not spend more time in searching for a watersource before you put the dinner on to cook.

CAMP-SITES

One of the hardest things about finding a place to camp is to find the owner of the land, and get his permission before you pitch there. Every bit of England is owned by someone, and you will be the more welcome for asking for permission to camp. There is no getting away from the fact however that in many cases there will be no one around for miles in the place you want to put up your tent, and that by so doing, you will be technically guilty of trespass. There are times when the risk of detection will be greater than others; for the good of all other backpackers, it makes sense to get permission when you can, and to be extra careful about how you camp if you have not been able to find the landowner, so that at the very least, he will not be able to take you to task for irresponsible behaviour while on his land. Pitching anywhere without permission is the wrong thing to do, whatever we think at the time, so for the purposes of this particular flight of fancy, I will assume that you have met the landowner and got his permission to pitch on his land.

The wind is getting up again, and suddenly it seems like the end of the walking day. You look for the flattest place you can see, which is sheltered from the prevailing wind, and you check it over for stones, sticks, thistles and anything which might puncture the thin groundsheet of the tent. You certainly don't want to be at the bottom of a valley, or even too near a stream, as it is always colder in those places. Preferably you will find a place where the rising sun will warm you, and dry out the tent fast, but this is real luxury, and not always to be found unless you make a point of laying-in the site by compass bearing. If you have to accept a slope, make sure that you sleep with your head uphill. Any other variation will leave you sleeping very badly, if at all.

PITCHING THE TENT
When you have cleared the ground where you will put down the tent, estimate where the main pegs will go, and stick a peg in the ground at each point. then take out the main parts of the tent from your pack, and assemble the poles, laying them in their rough positions. If you have a tent whose flysheet can be pitched first, you can start by pegging the tail down into wind so that whatever else happens, the wind will not tear the tent out of your hands and blow it into the next valley. Put in pegs in approximately the right positions by lifting the flysheet as though the poles were holding it up, and guess where the guylines should reach too. A little practice will make you very accurate at this, and once the guylines are pegged, you can insert the poles and erect the tent, confident that you will at least have a "shape" on it, no matter how hard the wind may blow. Once the outer tent is up, you can adjust the pegs until it sets just right, and everything else may be done under shelter.

Inside the flysheet there will be a marvellous sense of stillness and calm, where the air seems warmer, and the noise less. In this haven of rest you pin your inner tent down, hooking its tapes up to the flysheet to give you the usual draught-free, breathable "people packet" that a good inner ought to be. Once your portable home is up, you can slide the piece of thin closed-cell foam under the groundsheet, or even put it down inside the tent, to give the effect of having a fitted carpet with underlay. It also stops the heather stubs, twigs and small stones from puncturing the groundsheet when you are lying on it. Out comes the sleeping bag, to be put to loft on the thicker bit of closed-cell foam that will serve as your mattress. Then, if the weather permits, you can set up the kitchen outside and get the supper on to cook.

When you are really adept at putting up the tent, you can set up the kitchen before you erect your shelter, so that by the time your portable home is up, the meal is ready. This knack takes a bit of practice however, as even with pre-cooked, tinned food, there will always be a bit of stirring to be done, and you can't always drop what you are doing to go over and stir the pot.

If the rain has begun by now, get into the tent and sit on the groundsheet, taking care not to put your boots on the inner tent. Under shelter, but leaving a lot of ventilation open, you can prepare the evening meal; take great care when lighting the stove that no flame comes into contact with the nylon of the tent, or you will have a nasty accident coming. Nylon melts and drips; if it drips on you, you'll be a long time wearing it. In any case leave plenty of room around the stove, for sheer ease of movement. Once you are sitting in the front of the tent, try not to move too much or you may knock something over. Before you light the stove, lay out what you will need for the meal and have it all ready to hand. This is where the gaiters are so useful, in providing a clean inside area for putting the spoons, pot-grabbers, tin opener, lighter and food packets on.

When you are starting to teach yourself good backpacking habits, try to do the cooking in daylight. You must know what you are doing before you try cooking by candle or torch-light. If there is a draught coming round the bottom of the flysheet, put something in the way to stop it; you can use your raingear, or even your boots or pack. Some backpackers like to leave their packs outside the tent covered with a large plastic bag. This leaves the pack weatherproof, and gives more room inside the tent, but I generally bring my pack inside, unload it, and put the empty pack down the side of the tent between the inner and flysheet.

When you have eaten, wash the pots so that they are all clean for the morning. The easy way is to boil a little water in one dirty pot, with a bit of soap powder in it. When the water is hot, rinse the water round with a J-cloth, using the same water for the other pots in turn. Tip out the dirty water carefully, under a clump of grass, and never wash the pots in a running stream. Cold water will clean pots just as well as hot, but always take pots away from the stream so that no food or soap floats off down the hill.

SETTLING-DOWN

By now, the unaccustomed exercise and all the fresh air will be starting to make you sleepy. You've walked a fair way, pitched a tent, cooked a meal and eaten it, and done the washing up. Now is the time to check over the tentpegs, have a walk around the site for any last-minute looks at the weather or the view in the darkening twilight and then get back into the tent. Once inside for the night, you peel off the clothing you've worn all day, and put it into the stuffsack of the sleeping bag to act as a pillow and to keep it free from condensation. If you have brought a sleeping suit, or a change of clothes, put them on. The feel of clean, dry clothing will be luxurious, and will warm you quickly as you get into the well-fluffed sleeping bag that has been lofting ever since you finished pitching the tent. Your trousers will do nicely as an extension of the foam mat you lie on, and will insulate your legs and feet from the ground's chill. Once you are in the sleeping bag, you can light your candle and put it in a cookpot well away from the wall of the tent, and suddenly the whole fragile structure will glow with warmth and light. Perhaps a last brew before sleep, or a look at the map for tomorrow's route, or even read a paper-back book; some walkers keep a diary, and this is the time to write it up, and consider the events of the day. Whatever you do, there will come that moment when you blow out the candle, and snuggle into the sleeping bag, letting the tiredness carry you into sleep.

Despite the differences in one's sleep pattern between a bed at home and a bed in a tent, I always manage to get a good night's rest when I am in the fresh air. Morning seems to come all too soon, and the bright day gives one the urge to be up and moving again. One of the backpacking luxuries though, is having breakfast in bed, and having muesli with you makes this easy. A pan of water makes both tea and warm milk (when the dried milk is mixed into the muesli), and then the stove can be turned off and allowed to cool till the time comes to pack it away for the day's hike. A bit of sugar makes the muesli more palatable, and I frequently add this when I bag up the food at home. There is not much washing-up to be done, and if you gauge it right, there will be some warm water left over for this purpose.

PACKING-UP

Problems of packing-up are only aggravated by bad weather outside. In such a case, the flysheet is left standing until the last, when everything else has been put into the pack. You then don your raingear, and strike the flysheet, putting it into the pack under the top flap, where it will not come into contact with the dry gear in the main compartment. Some lightweight tents come complete with little bags for poles, pegs, inner and flysheet, and as these are made of tent material, they are waterproof. These are ideal for wet tents, which can be rolled tightly and compressed into less pack space this way.

If the weather is good though, packing can proceed after the tent is taken down, as the flysheet may need drying out on the inside, and the inner could do with an airing. Turn the fly over on the ground, pegging it down if necessary to stop it from blowing away. Hang the sleeping bag inside out to air, to avoid that clammy feeling that an un-aired bag has when you get into it at night. If the grass is wet, but it is not actually raining, the indispensable gaiters will save your trousers from a soaking as you walk. Put the final bits into the pack, make sure the trail snacks are handy, have a last look around to make sure you have not left anything, like a tentpeg stuck in the ground, and move off.

It is best not to start off too fast. It will take a mile or so to get into the rythm of the walk, and to let the pack settle down on your back. Soon the stride will become looser and more automatic, and once again you begin to cover the day's miles with ease. You have slept well, you have a good breakfast inside you, and it's already a great day. What more could you want? There's no pressure, no telephone, no television, no motorcars, no newspapers full of gloomy news. There's just the track in front of you, rising, and the wind at your back.

Keep right on moving. There's a long way to go today.

Chapter 9

HAZARDS

Granted, it's not always like that. When you branch away from everyday things, you expect the new things to be different or there'd be no point in getting away at all. But possibly some of the different things could be unpleasant ones, and it is as well to be prepared for some of them. The backpacker with a life-support system in his pack is well equipped to cope with most mountain emergencies, but maybe there will be the day when you leave the pack in the tent while you go off on a ramble to look at the other side of the hill. Down comes the mist, it starts to rain, and if you're not actually lost, at the least you are temporarily unsure of your position.

The rain can chill you, if you don't have some form of raingear. Too much chilling, and your body will no longer be able to produce all the heat you need to combat the chill. Your body temperature will drop, you will feel tired and cold, with cramps in your limbs, your speech will slur and you will start to do irrational things; you may have hallucinations or abnormal vision, and eventually you will collapse into coma. Observe these symptoms as they result in Hypothermia, the mountain killer. At the first symptom you must get the casualty out of the wind, warm him up, and make him rest. The best cure though, is prevention.

As conditions change in the hills so rapidly, you should always take a minimum emergency kit with you that will help stave off the symptoms outlined above. Extra clothing such as a sweater or down jacket will help retain your body heat under raingear, high-energy rations will help your body to go on producing warmth, a map and compass will assist you to find your way to your camp, a torch will help you to look at the map and compass, and a first-aid kit and a whistle will let you treat injuries and attract other assistance if nececssary. All the above will fit into a small beltpack or backpack and should be considered essentials for mountain walking. Even if you are backpacking in the lowlands and could get to safety quickly if the weather changes, it is good practice to carry these items as a *matter of habit*, even on country walks. Get into the habit of safety.

FIGURE 12

BACK PACKERS
COUNTRY

THE HIGHLANDS

CHEVIOTS

PENNINES

YORKS MOORS

PEAK
DISTRICT

SNOWDONIA

BRECON
BEACONS

EXMOOR

THE RIDGEWAY

THE DOWNS

DARTMOOR

FIRST AID KIT

Your first-aid kit should contain as a minimum, some plasters for blisters or cuts, some gauze or lint to use as dressings on a wound, some bandages to cover the wound, aspirin for headaches and other pain and some antiseptic cream. I also carry Optone eye-drops to wash dust out of my eyes, anti-histamine spray in hay-fever time, some salt-tablets, waterpurifying tablets, safety pins and a needle and thread.

It's no good having a compass and a map with you if you can't read and use them. You can teach yourself map-reading and compass-work by buying a good book on the subject and practicing the exercises in it. (The Spurbook of Map and Compass is a good one and a full list of Spur Outdoor titles appears at the front of this book). Practice whenever possible in good conditions, so that use of the compass is instinctive, and if an emergency happens, you won't have that mind-stopping moment when you realise that not only do you not know where you are, but you can't find the right direction in which to keep going.

Most backpackers go into the country hoping to be alone with themselves or just their chosen companions. They don't really want to be reminded that other people are there too, and they don't want to intrude their own presence on others. They dress accordingly in country colours, in quiet browns and greens that will blend with the countryside rather than stand out vividly in contrast. Bright orange and red garments may be fine for mountaineers, but for quiet passage through the hills, I prefer toned-down hues. I don't believe in the theory that I would be "safer" if I wear brightly-coloured clothing; I don't go into the hills expecting a need to be rescued. Although I am aware of the possibility that something might happen, I take as many precautions against it actually accurring as I can, on the basis that application of common sense and common self-preservation will prevent an accident, and that prevention is better than permanently to carry the means of the cure. Having said all that, I still carry something very bright and attention-getting inside my pack, and I still carry my whistle to attract help if I need it.

SAFETY ON ROADS

One aspect of safety that does affect the backpacker is visibility at night, if moving along country roads. Here a strip or piece of dayglo orange reflecting tape on the back of the pack, or a torch that straps on the arm, showing a white light before and a red light to the rear, is a safety asset that cannot be criticised. In such circumstances, it is part of common sense to wish to be seen. Always where possible walk facing the on-coming traffic, then you can dodge if they don't.

Other hazards include the weather, fire and just plain accident. When planning a trip, plan to carry enough gear to cope with the worst possible conditions you can anticipate at that season. Learn to read the weather so that you can make an educated estimate of the next day's weather without getting a radio forecast. Don't just plough on blindly into a mountain storm. Don't stay high when there is lightning about; Get as far downhill as you can, as fast as you can, and keep off exposed ridges; avoid trees, small hollows, caves, walls and isolated buildings.

We have discussed the dangers of fire in a tent caused by the stove. Precautions to be taken with stoves include never filling a hot stove with petrol; never relighting a hot stove inside the tent; never allowing a stove to over-heat—this is particularly applicable to petrol stoves which have a pressure release valve, which blows out at a preset temperature, and which will emit a stream of ignited petrol vapour like a torch if fuel tank pressure goes too high by becoming too warm; never lighting a gas stove by turning on the gas and holding a match to it—always light the match first, hold it to the burner and then turn on the gas; in short, know your gear, and know the hazards connected with it.

Accidents are largely caused by carelessness. Prevention is easier than cure. Try not to get over-confident in your own powers of endurance or walking skills. Anyone can make a mistake, but it's *where* you make that mistake that can mean the difference between life and death—a cut finger or a cut artery.

Remember this, go backpacking, and enjoy yourself.

Chapter 10

WHERE TO GO

We have that incalculably valuable asset in Britain, a vast network of public footpaths. These allow access to areas that no other transport than feet can really reach. No matter where these footpaths go however, it is always across someone's land, and the fact that the path is a public right of way does not infer the right to camp along it. Make it a rule that you will always seek permission to pitch your camp, and you will be in less danger of falling foul of outraged landowners.

The public footpaths will let you start your backpacking career close to home, but the planned Long-Distance paths cover huge stretches of the wilder parts of the country, and present the walking camper with a tough challenge. My advice is that you should not try to tackle any of them without some training in basic backpacking first. Treat the Pennine Way as a graduation course, if you like, but not as an introduction to Backpacking. It will give you a greater sense of achievement if you can plan a few routes of your own, without the benefit of the Countryside Commission. Try to map a route, and get permission to camp from the farmers whose land your route covers, and you will be on your way to regular practice in backpacking. At least you will then have some quiet, private pitches of your own, where you can go to practice new aspects of equipment, or techniques you may have read about. No matter where you live, it should be possible to build up an area in which you feel completely at home, in familiar surroundings; only then will you be truly fit to move into unknown country.

One of the best ways to see various bits of the country in the company of other backpackers is to join the Backpackers Club. The address is c/o Eric Gurney, National Organiser, Backpackers' Club, 20 St. Michael's Road, Tilehurst, Reading. This organisation exists to be a fellowship of walking campers, and a voice to speak for their interests. Although it is sometimes described as a "club for un-clubbable people", it organises training weekends in areas such as the Brecon Beacons, the Peak District, the Cheviots, the Highlands, the South Downs and the Berkshire Ridgeway, so that new members may meet the Club, and walk and camp with other members without worrying about where to pitch, or whether there will be water, or any of the other minor worries that beset the beginner. Opinions on all sorts of equipment can be sought without the feeling that a salesman is telling you something, and a user's opinion on an item you have been thinking of getting is very valuable. If you feel that organisations are not for you, then the whole of Britain is open to you as a walker's country. he landscape is so varied that you can virtually take your pick of moorland, sea-coast, hills or valleys, rivers or mountain ridges. The remotest areas as far as population is concerned, are in the Highlands of Scotland, the mountains of Wales (except Snowdonia in the tourist season) the Yorkshire moors, and the Pennines. In these places it is possible to move for days without seeing anyone else. Don't go to such places in the shooting season though; the rearing and shooting of game birds in the uplands is now a country industry, whatever your feelings on such things. If we as backpackers want the country people to respect our rights of travel across their land, we must equally be seen to respect their traditions and way of life in turn.

For this very reason, the backpacker must be a conservationist. We, above all other visitors to the countryside, must be seen and known to be an asset in the country, rather than a liability. The Country Code explains the minimum level of personal conduct in the country; it is the charter of the Backpackers Club. I say "minimum" level, because one should always try to do a bit more than the injunctions of the Code, and we ought to know the reasons behind the rules that are laid down there. The removal of litter is vital, for example, because of the grave danger of its being eaten by a farm animal with fatal consequences to that animal, and financial loss to the owner. To leave a gate open may allow a beast to stray into the road to cause an accident, or at least a traffic hazard; it also inflicts a time penalty on those who have to round the animal up later.

More than the Country Code alone is needed in our approach to the country areas where we go for our leisure. We need to nurture a deep sense of responsibilty to the countryside, to cherish what has been handed down to us from the past, and to try to conserve it for our children so that they may enjoy what we are enjoying. If we can be seen and recognised by the country-dwellers as quiet and responsible visitors, we will always be welcomed there when we come as backpackers.

I hope that this book has helped you in some way to be a backpacker, and to show you how to live out of your pack. I hope that some day we will meet, out there in the "green bits".